Lost In Indiana

Discovering Strange and Historic Places in The Hoosier State

•ETAOIN PUBLISHING•
www.etaoinpublishing.com

HURON
PHOTO.COM

Publisher: Etaoin Publishing and Huron Photo LLC
             Saginaw, MI
             www.EtaoinPublishing.com
             www.HuronPhoto.com

Printed in the United States of America

Paperback ISBN 978-1-955474-10-8
Hardcover ISBN 978-1-955474-11-5
Ebook ISBN 978-1-955474-12-2

A Lost In The States Book
www.LostInTheStates.com

Introduction

To many people, Indiana is a state known for corn fields and auto racing. The Hoosier State does have a lot of farmland and a famous racetrack, but it also has a fascinating history. Traveling the backroads through small towns, big cities, farmland and forests, there are plenty of historic sites and unique places to visit. Some are well-known and important, like Abraham Lincoln's boyhood home, and others are forgotten with time but still noteworthy. From tragic events to heroic people, Indiana has a lot to see on a road trip around the Hoosier State.

It's fun to go to the popular tourist destinations like Shipshewana or French Lick, but shopping and eating can get expensive. If you are on a limited budget, there are plenty of fun and interesting places to visit that are free or cost a small donation. Many parks and historical sites offer the chance for a getaway and are free to explore. If you are willing to be a little adventurous, cemeteries can be fascinating places to visit and also have a lot of stories and history to share. If you are fortunate to be in good physical condition, the forests give people a chance to hike, and some of the trails lead past some amazing places.

This book is not intended to be a "bucket list" of all the things you should see and do in Indiana but instead, stories of places, people and things that I found interesting as I traversed the state. Each story in this book is an independent tale about a specific location in the state. You can read them in any order. I do my best to give accurate locations, although some places do not have a specific address, so I give a description of where it can be found. Most places are open to the public and located on public property, but be sure to follow any posted rules, and please be respectful of places you visit. Some places are privately owned and are sometimes opened to the public. Although they may not be accessible, they do have an interesting story that I wanted to share, and I hope that you will be considerate of the owners' privacy.

Contents

Chapter 1
Southern Indiana

Chapter 2
Central Indiana

Chapter 3
Northern Indiana

Chapter 1
Southern Indiana

Myers Cabin

In the Muscatatuck National
Wildlife Refuge
The cabin is Located on 475 S. Road
Seymour, IN 47274
GPS Coordinates:
38.91444662313615, -85.80315623986893

East of the town of Seymour is the Muscatatuck National
Wildlife Refuge. About five miles down a dusty gravel road
deep within the refuge is an old log cabin. It was built in the
early 1880s and is a link to Indiana's pioneering past. Louis

2

Myers built the log cabin for his family using logs and materials from the surrounding forests. They farmed the land for survival and built a barn along with a chicken coop, which still stands behind the home. Louis' wife was the last person to reside in the home; she died in 1948. At the time of her death, the cabin was sheathed in siding and looked more like a modern home. The Muscatatuck National Wildlife Refuge was established in 1966 and encompassed the land that the home stood on. The siding was removed, and the home has been restored and furnished to the way it would have been in the early 1900s.

The house was not the only structure to stand in the area. At one time it was a thriving farming community with several homes, a church, schoolhouse and sawmill. In time, all of the buildings were moved or torn down other than the old Myers' cabin. During Prohibition, the remote community was a haven for illegal alcohol and got the nickname of "Moonshine Valley".

A few miles north of the cabin off N. County 1000 Road is the Barkman Cemetery where some of the Myers family are laid to rest along with other citizens of the old farming community.

Tunnel Mill

The old chimney still standing among the trees.

Park at Baldwin Cemetery on
W. County Rd. 60 S.
North Vernon, IN 47265
38.9756083817649, -85.60777033756138

The Muscatatuck River winds its way around the town of
Vernon in southern Indiana. The river makes several twists and
turns through the rocky terrain, and it is just south of town
where Ebenezer Baldwin built a mill in the early 1800s. On a
spot along the river where it made a loop, he connected the

4

river by digging a tunnel through the shale. A dam was built along the river and the water rushed through the tunnel, powering the mill. It was an incredible feat of engineering at the time, and farmers came by horseback with sacks of grain and corn to be ground by the mill.

Over time, the mill became obsolete and was no longer used. The dam had been removed or just deteriorated to the point that it no longer held back the river. Except for a small corner of the wall and the chimney, the mill had been removed.

The tunnel through the rocky terrain that powered the mill.

The tunnel and mill ruins can still be seen after taking a short hike through the dense woods along the Muscatatuck River. The trail to the mill starts at the back of the Baldwin Cemetery. A sign marks the start of the trail and reminds visitors to be careful of the rocky terrain. Be sure to heed the warning, which is there for good reason. I had great difficulty stumbling around on the rocks and boulders. I recommend taking a walking stick with you to keep your balance. It is really easy to fall or twist an ankle on all the jagged and loose rocks in the old riverbed.

The town of Vernon is one of the oldest cities in Indiana. The entire town is listed in the National Register of Historic Places.

Initial Point

E. Pivot Point Rd.
Paoli, IN 47454
38.47009940038384, -86.45506615779725

South of Paoli in the Hoosier National Forest is the Initial Point. It is the spot where the state of Indiana was initially surveyed from. In 1805, Ebenezer Buckingham Jr. placed a wooden post at the intersection of the Base Line with the 2nd Principal Meridian. The mark is where all Indiana township and range sections are derived from. In 1866, the post was replaced with a stone marked "S 31" for section 31.

In 1968, a group of people from the Indiana Society of Professional Land Surveyors, Indiana County Surveyors Association, and citizens of Paoli purchased eighteen acres of land surrounding the Initial Point. They deeded the property over to the Forest Service and worked together to protect and maintain the site.

The stone marker is surrounded by a triangular wooden fence. A trail leads visitors down into a small valley. It is a narrow footpath and about a quarter mile to reach the site. It is not extremely difficult to hike, but it is not ADA accessible and you need to be in good health to make the short trip down and back up the valley that it is located in. I highly recommend using bug spray to thwart off the many mosquitoes that you will encounter.

A memorial marker dedicated to the initial point and the people who surveyed it was erected in front of the court house in Paoli.

Jasper City Mill

164 Third Ave.
Jasper, IN 47546
38.38737422190254, -86.92766231237016

The Patoka River flows through the southern Indiana city of Jasper. Along the banks of the river near downtown is an old-looking grist mill called the Jasper City Mill. It may look old, but it was constructed in 2009 using old and historic components. It is the third mill to stand on the site.

The first mill was constructed in 1817. Jasper made an ideal site because the flour it produced could be shipped by flatboat down the Patoka River to the Wabash and Ohio Rivers and as far south as New Orleans, Louisiana. It is believed that a young Abraham Lincoln came with his father Thomas to the mill in 1828. They bartered goods for a sack of cornmeal for their family farm located to the south of Jasper. Lincoln's boyhood home is now a National Historic Memorial.

The second mill was constructed in 1865. The grinding stones were replaced with rollers to increase the output of flour. In the 1930s the lower level of the mill was damaged, and it stopped grinding grain. It stood for nearly a century, mainly used as a warehouse for grain and feed after the 1930s, when it was torn down in 1964 after being damaged in a flood. The property was turned over to the city of Jasper and used as a park.

In 2009, a new mill was built using a 150-year-old water wheel, shafts and gears from a mill in Virginia. The mill stones are approximately 200 years old and came from France. The building now serves as both a history center and visitors center. It continues to grind small amounts of grain to show visitors the inner workings of an historic water-powered mill.

The mill is also a great place to park for a hike along the Jasper Riverwalk trail that follows next to the Patoka River.

Constitution Elm

200 W. High St.
Corydon, IN 47112
38.2135341934935, -86.12734479326656

In a residential neighborhood in the town of Corydon is an old tree trunk protected by a stone monument. It looks rather strange, but if you know the importance of the old tree, it makes perfect sense. In 1816, President James Madison signed into law a bill that created the state of Indiana. Delegates met in Corydon to write the state's first Constitution. Corydon was chosen as the first capital because it was centrally located to most of the state's population at the time. As they began work on the new document in June, the building they were working in became unbearably hot. The group decided to move outside and work under the branches of a large elm tree.

The Constitutional Convention lasted 19 days. On the last day, June 29, 1816, the state constitution was adopted by a majority vote. It included several progressive laws, like a ban on slavery and the first mandate for funding public schools in the country. The Constitutional Elm became a symbol of Indiana's statehood, and the tree has been honored by Hoosiers over the years.

In the 1920s, the historic tree was ravaged by Dutch Elm disease. Efforts were made to try and save it, but eventually they failed. To preserve what they could for future generations, the local chapter of the Daughters of the American Revolution had the branches cut off and sold pieces for souvenirs. A stone monument was built around the remaining trunk. Over the years, several attempts have been made to preserve it from dry rot and decay. In the early days, it was covered with coal tar. More recently, since 2016, the Indiana State Museum has been working to preserve the historic tree or at least what remains of it.

Culbertson Mansion

914 E. Main St.
New Albany, IN 47150
38.286721282508125,-85.81281825049489

The town of New Albany is located along the Ohio River across from Louisville, Kentucky. The Ohio River Scenic Byway passes through the town. It has several historic houses and buildings, but a three-story golden yellow mansion on

Main Street stands out among them. It was the home of William Culbertson. At the time he constructed it in 1867, Culbertson was believed to be the richest man in Indiana. He came to New Albany from Pennsylvania at the age of 21. He took a job as a dry goods clerk. With the knowledge he learned as a clerk, he started his own dry goods store, which prospered. He died in 1892 at the age of 78 and had a net worth of $3.5 million dollars, which would be worth about $61 million today.

He built his magnificent home in 1867 which cost about $120,000 to construct. The 20,000 square foot mansion has twenty-five rooms and carved rosewood staircases. The original tin roof was imported from Scotland. No expense was spared, and he had artists hand paint detailed and ornate designs on the ceiling and walls.

After Culbertson's death, he willed the home to his third wife, who auctioned off the house and contents in 1899 to John McDonald, also a resident of New Albany, for $7,100. After McDonald, the American Legion obtained it from his daughter. The Legion made extensive changes to the mansion, making it more suitable for a meeting place. After changing owners a few more times, the old mansion was to be demolished to make room for a new gas station. A local historical group raised the funds to purchase the historic home and had it placed on the National Register of Historic Places. In 1976, it became a part of the Indiana State Museum and Historic Sites.

Events are held throughout the year to raise funds to restore the historic home. The most popular event is during the fall when the carriage house is converted into a haunted house staffed with 100 volunteers. Info on events and tours can be found at www.indianamuseum.org/historic-sites/culbertson-mansion/.

Nike Missile Site

 On IN-262 about 2 miles south of US-50
Dillsboro, IN 47018
39.001645478519386, -85.03423062214662

South of Dillsboro in a remote part of Southeastern Indiana is an old abandoned faded green building surrounded by chain link fencing topped with barbed wire. The entrance from the road has an old guard shack that looks as if it has not been manned for a long time. Privately owned and closed off to the public, it was one of many Nike missile sites operated by the U.S. military during the Cold War.

At the end of World War II, a new system was needed to defend against enemy aircraft strikes. With the invention of jet fighter planes, conventional anti-aircraft guns were insufficient. Project Nike stationed a series of missiles around the county in case of attack. Four missile sites were placed in the vicinity of Cincinnati and Dayton. Three sites are in Ohio, and one in Indiana near Dillsboro. The sites became operational in the 1960s and remained active until 1970. All four sites were sold off and are now privately owned. They are a reminder of a time during the Cold War when we thought we could thwart off a nuclear attack with bases in the midwest.

Benjamin Schenk Mansion

206 W. Turnpike St.
Vevay, IN 47043
38.75066572586158, -85.07347246442755

The small town of Vevay sits along the Ohio River between Louisville, Kentucky and Cincinnati, Ohio. The beautiful little river town has a historic downtown surrounded by average midwestern homes. The one home that stands out is an enormous second empire style brick mansion that stands on a hillside overlooking the community of Vevay. The home known as the Schenck Mansion was built in 1874 by Benjamin Franklin Schenck, the son of the "Hay King" Ulysses Schenck.

In the early 1800s, many Europeans came to the Ohio River Valley in the hopes of starting a new life in the United States. Many Swiss families came to the area around Vevay, and the county was given the name Switzerland County. In 1817, Ulysses Schenck emigrated from Switzerland to Vevay and set up a mercantile business selling goods to local farmers. Realizing there was money to be made in transporting hay downriver, he purchased a steamboat to ship the feed grown by local farmers. As business grew along with his wealth, he became known as the Hay King.

With the money gained from his father's business, Benjamin Schenk built his grand home on the hillside overlooking the town. Tragically, he died two years after construction began in 1874 and was never able to live in the completed home. His widow and children lived in the home a few years before moving away. The house on the hill sat empty for decades until the family donated the home to the Indiana Baptist Convention in 1923. The mansion was given back to the family in 1928 and then sold to the Wiseman family in 1945. The home had changed owners several times over the decades, and the upper floors had been divided up into apartments. In the late 90s, Jerry and Lisa Fisher purchased the home and renovated it into a bed and breakfast. The new owners fixed up the old mansion, bringing it back to the grandeur it once had when it was originally built. In 2020, the home was sold to tattoo artist Kat Von D, who starred on the TV show LA Ink. She is using it as a private residence.

There are rumors of the home being haunted. One of the stories claims that the land that the mansion was built on originally had a home on it that burned down. The owners of the home were trapped inside and burned up with the house, and their spirits still roam the property. The fact that Benjamin Schenck died before the home was completed also lends one to believe his spirit still haunts the home he constructed. I am not sure any of it is true, but it is a beautiful historic house along the Ohio River.

The house is closed to the public, but you can see it from the road. You can get a better view of it during the winter months when the leaves are gone from the trees.

Gus's Rocket Monument

407 S. 6th St.
Mitchell, IN 47446
38.729394592457176, -86.4711557923049

Looking at the moon in the night sky, it is hard to imagine that United States astronauts walked on the moon. It took great sacrifices to achieve the impossible, including time, money and lives. One of those lives was Virgil "Gus" Grissom. He was born and raised in Mitchell, Indiana, and a memorial in the shape of a rocket stands in his hometown.

Born in 1926, he enlisted in the U.S. Army Air Force during World War II. After the war, he went to Purdue University where he graduated with a degree in mechanical engineering. He re-enlisted in the U.S. Air Force, earning his pilot's wings in 1951, and flew 100 combat missions during the Korean War. He attended the U.S. Air Force Institute of Technology, earned a bachelor's degree in aeromechanics and became a test pilot for the military.

He was chosen as one of the Mercury Seven astronauts and was the second American sent into space by NASA. On January 27, 1967, Grissom and astronauts Ed White and Roger

Chaffe were in the capsule on the launchpad preparing for an Apollo mission. Their capsule caught fire, and the three astronauts died before they could escape from the smoke and flames.

The memorial dedicated to Grissom in Mitchell was built where the grade school he once attended had stood. The walls surrounding the memorial were made using the bricks from the old school building.

He received his nickname when his friend was reading his name on a scorecard upside down and misread "Griss" as "Gus".

Whispers Estate

 714 W. Warren St.
Mitchell, IN 47446
38.733504122568554, -86.4745058067034

North of downtown Mitchell on a block of modest homes is a rather unassuming two-story house. It has a wrought iron fence and a pair of stone angel statues in front of it. Looking at it from the outside, you would assume it was just another ordinary midwestern home. Inside, the owner claims strange paranormal events happen, making it one of the most haunted locations in the Hoosier State.

Known as the Whispers Estate, it was built in 1894. Dr. John Gibbons purchased the home in 1899 and used the lower floor as his office, where he saw patients. Dr. Gibbons and his wife had adopted several orphaned children and were well respected in the community. Their ten-year-old daughter Rachel was severely burned by a fire she started in the parlor. Two days later, she died in her upstairs bedroom. The Gibbon's ten-month-old daughter Elizabeth died in the home from a mysterious illness. Dr. Gibbon's wife Jessie died of pneumonia in the same bedroom that Elizabeth passed away in.

The house, having seen its share of tragedy over the decades, is said to be cursed by some of its former residents. Some people have claimed to see the spirit of a little girl roaming the house, possibly that of Rachel. They also have heard the sounds of heavy breathing and coughing in the master bedroom where Jessie died from pneumonia. They say the door knob on the closet door jiggles on its own and the door mysteriously opens. The home is known as Whispers Estate because guests have heard strange voices whispering in their ears.

The current owners operate the home as an inn where guests can spend the night and possibly experience strange happenings themselves. You can learn more at their website: www.whispersestate.godaddysites.com.

Joe Palooka Statue

109 Main St.
Oolitic, IN 47451
38.90099919354445, -86.52640487984189

The town of Oolitic can be found between Bloomington and French Lick. There you will find a strange looking statue of a man in a cape wearing boxing attire next to the Oolitic Town Hall on Main Street.

It is a statue of comic strip hero Joe Palooka created in 1930 by Ham Fisher. Joe Palooka was a fictional boxing character with a big heart and a defender of the "little guy". At its peak in the 1940s and 50s, the comic strip was syndicated in over nine hundred newspapers. It gained widespread popularity during World War II when the strip showed Joe Palooka fighting the Nazis on a weekly basis. Movies and TV shows were created about the lovable boxing champ. By the 1980s, the comic strip's popularity had waned, and the final strip ran in newspapers in 1984.

How did this statue come to stand in Oolitic? Indiana Limestone Company wanted to celebrate their decades of providing limestone for the nation's buildings, including the

Empire State Building in New York City. The company thought it would be a great fit to have a statue of the fictional boxing champion unveiled at its company celebration in 1948 in the nearby town of Bedford. The statue stood on a hill overlooking IN-37, but Joe's recognition faded and it was in danger of being vandalized. In 1984, the statue was moved to Oolitic, where it stands today next to the town hall.

The town of Oolitic was platted in 1896 by the Bedford Quarries Company. Oolitic is a type of limestone found in Indiana. Oolitic is the opposing basketball team during the season opener in the film *Hoosiers*.

House of the Singing Winds

4220 T C Steele Rd.
Nashville, IN 47448
39.131658091838084, -86.34842176443173

Between Bloomington and Nashville, Indiana is the T.C. Steele
State Historic Site. It was the home of one of Indiana's most
famous artists. Theodore Clement "T.C." Steele was born in
1847 in Gosport, Indiana. Steele began formal art training as a

boy at the Waveland Collegiate Institute (Waveland Academy). When he was sixteen, he began attending Asbury College (now DePauw University) in Greencastle, Indiana. Steele also studied briefly in Chicago, Illinois and Cincinnati, Ohio before returning to Indiana to make a living painting portraits on commission.

In 1870, Steele married his first wife Elizabeth, and for a short time they lived in southern Michigan and then moved to Indianapolis. Elizabeth died of tuberculosis in 1899. Eight years later, he married his second wife Selma in 1907, and they built a home in the secluded Indiana woods in Brown County. They named their home House of the Singing Winds because of the breezes that blew through the porch. It is here that Steele built a studio and painted many bright and colorful Indiana landscapes. In December 1925, Steele suffered a heart attack and died the following June. Selma continued to live in the house until she died in 1845. Before her death, she donated the home, studio and 211 acres to the Indiana Department of Natural Resources, which now operates the property as an historic site. Visitors can tour the home and studio and see some of T.C. Steele's artwork on display.

A Town's Tombstone

Elkinsville Road
a few miles west of Story
39.07428952311196, -86.26252365244834

Elkinsville Road winds its way deep into the Hoosier National Forest. Near the end of the road you will find a stone marker for "The Town That Was". It stands like a tombstone for the town of Elkinsville.

The town was founded in 1860 by William Elkin. The rural farming village survived in the beautiful remote wilderness for about a century. It never grew into a large city, but it did have several houses along with a church, school, blacksmith and a post office.

As the population of Bloomington grew, it was necessary to have a large source of drinking water. In the 1960s, the U.S. Army Corps of Engineers decided to dam the Salt Creek and create Lake Monroe water reservoir. They determined that the town of Elkinsville would be in the floodplain and be underwater. In 1964, the government, using eminent domain, acquired the private property belonging to the citizens and businesses of Elkinsville. Most of the houses and buildings

were moved or demolished before the reservoir was created. When Lake Monroe was created and the water stopped rising, the land where the town of Elkinsville remained above water. The elevation of the town had been miscalculated, and it was not necessary to disband the town, but by then it was too late, and the town had already been removed from the Indiana forest.

In 2003, the former residents raised enough funds to erect a stone to remember the town. On it is a poem: "That day we moved, we'll never forget, as goodbyes were said and the sun set. Never again in these hills we'll roam, but in our hearts this is always home."

The few homes and buildings that stand in the former town have been sold back into private hands. The area offers hiking and wilderness to explore, but please do not trespass around any of the buildings.

The Oldest Building in Indiana

 1 Harrison St.
Vincennes, IN 47591
38.68556389639316, -87.52512866442966

The city of Vincennes sits along the Wabash River that makes up the western boundary between Indiana and Illinois. It is the oldest city in Indiana and is the home to the oldest building in the state. Known as the "Red House", the two-story building was used as the first territorial capitol.

In 1800, the Northwest Territory was divided into two territories, the eastern region called the Ohio Territory and the western region called the Indiana Territory. Vincennes had been a French trading post along the banks of the Wabash River, and it became the first territorial capital. A two-story building built in 1805 was a tailor shop. In 1811, the territorial government was divided into a two-house legislative system. At that point, the government moved into the "Red House", The lower level of the building held the nine-member House of Representatives and the upper level the Legislative Council. It was used as the first capital until Corydon was made the capital in 1813. The historic red building is the oldest building in Indiana and the oldest government building in the midwest.

It no longer stands on its original site and has been moved three times. It currently stands with three other historic buildings near President William Henry Harrison's mansion next to the campus of Vincennes University. The historic site is administered and maintained by Indiana State Museum and Historic Sites.

Story, Indiana

Corner of State road 135 and
Elkinsville road
39.09893369819012, -86.21412210202392

The town of Story is located in an isolated part of Indiana
near the southwestern boundary of Brown County State Park.
The charming little town is like a time capsule from days gone
by. The rustic old buildings and vintage advertising looks as if
it is something from a movie set, but it dates back to a time
when farming in the remote area was done by hard working
farmers.

The town got its start in 1851, when Dr. George Story was granted a land patent from President Willard Filmore. Dr. Story was a physician who lived in Ohio and came from a family in the lumbering business. He moved to his property in Indiana and built a home and an office where he practiced medicine. He built a few other buildings which attracted settlers to the area. In time the village grew to have two general stores, a church, a one-room schoolhouse, a grist mill, a sawmill, a slaughterhouse, a blacksmith's forge and a post office. In the 1880s, when the post office was established, it was officially given the name of Story.

The little town prospered in the early 1900s, but due to unseen circumstances, the town dwindled away to almost a ghost town. Farming the hilly and rocky area was a challenge, and when the Great Depression hit, many families gave up farming, selling their land to the government. When Lake Monroe was created by damming Salt Creek, the road that went through the town became a dead end, and travelers no longer passed through the old community.

In the 1970s, the town was sold and the historic general store and home was converted into an inn and restaurant. In 1999, the town once again fell on hard times and was sold at auction to new owners. Rick Hofstetter, an Indianapolis attorney and preservationist, and Frank Mueller, a German-born restaurateur, purchased the town and have managed to convert it into a delightful little town with an inn, cafe, BBQ joint and gift shop. It is a long, winding road from the popular tourist town of Nashville to get to Story, but it is worth the trip to visit this charming and historic place.

Since the 1970s, guests and employees have claimed to see an apparition of a woman wearing white robes and she has been given the name "the Blue Lady". She is believed to be the wife of Dr. George Story, and they say she has hypnotic blue eyes.

Lanier Mansion

601 W. 1st St.
Madison, IN 47250
38.735721285825235, -85.38714144897095

The historic town of Madison, Indiana is situated along the
Ohio River. The city has several historic buildings and homes
in the historic district, but a large dark yellow-colored mansion
stands out. The house was built by Madison banker and early
railroad investor James Franklin Doughty Lanier. Construction

began in 1840 and was completed in 1844. Lanier lived in the home for seven years before moving to New York City. He deeded the home to his son Alexander in 1861. And Alexander updated the home with gas lighting, indoor plumbing and a coal furnace.

The mansion remained in the Lanier family until 1917, when James' youngest son Charles donated the site to the Jefferson County Historical Society. About ten years later, in 1925, the home was given to the state, which opened it as a public museum. The grand old home has been painstakingly restored to its original condition. The interior and exterior were painted the original colors, and replica wall paper and carpeting were used throughout. The home is considered one of the finest examples of Greek Revival architecture in the United States.

The beautiful home is not without tragedy. James' wife died in the home two years after they moved into it. In 1836, shortly before the home was constructed, James Lanier's son little John James drowned in the Ohio River at the age of seven. Some say that they have seen the ghost of a lady, believed to be James' wife Elizabeth, in red in the home. Others have seen the spirit of a young boy in the garden walking towards the river. I wonder if the tragic events in Madison are what led James Lanier to move to New York.

During the fall months, visitors can take Ghost Tours of the Lanier Mansion along with a few nearby homes that are said to be haunted.

Abe's Boyhood Home

 3027 E. South St.
Lincoln City, IN 47552
38.12036842264624, -86.9969569634056

When looking at a list of the greatest United States presidents, Abraham Lincoln is near or at the top. Ending slavery and leading the country during the Civil War, his leadership through the challenging times has made him an iconic American figure. Growing up in Indiana shaped his character and beliefs.

He was born in Kentucky on his family farm, but due to land title challenges, his father lost everything he had worked for. In 1816, when Abraham was age seven, his family moved to southern Indiana, settling at the Little Pigeon Creek Community west of present day Santa Claus, Indiana. It is here that they built a log cabin and created a new family farm. It was not an easy life. Two years after moving from Kentucky, Lincoln's mother Nancy Hanks Lincoln died of milk sickness. It is a disease caused by eating dairy products from cows that ate the white snakeroot plant that has the toxin temetrol. She was buried on a hill south of the farm along with other settlers, including her aunt and uncle who died from the disease. The cemetery is now called Pioneer Cemetery.

In 1819, their father married Sarah Bush Johnston, a widow, of Elizabethtown, Kentucky, whom he had known when they lived there. Sarah raised Abraham like he was her own. He worked on the family farm and often went into town to listen to stories from the older men. He loved to read and borrowed books from anyone who would lend them. After fourteen years in southern Indiana, in March 1830, Thomas Lincoln moved his family to Central Illinois.

The cabin where the Lincolns lived is long gone, but the

location is marked by a bronze fireplace and foundation. Next to it is a recreation of Lincoln's farm, and visitors can experience what it was like for the family back in the days when young Abraham lived there. A trail leads from the farm to the visitors center and past the Pioneer Cemetery. The exact location of Nancy Hanks Lincon's burial is unknown, but a marker near the fence stands in her memory. It is surrounded by hundreds of pennies bearing her son's face tossed next to it by visitors.

In 1962, the U.S. Congress created the Lincoln Boyhood National Memorial. The site is maintained by the National Park Service.

First State Capitol Building

211 N. Capitol Ave.
Corydon, IN 47112
38.211638639796924, -86.12615254160076

Across from the town hall in Corydon on old Highway 135 is a two-story limestone building with a white cupola. This modest looking building served as Indiana's first state capitol building. It was constructed in 1813 to house the legislature of the

Indiana Territory after the capitol was moved from Vincennes to Corydon. At the time of its construction, it was the largest building in Indiana.

The lower floor of the statehouse was used by the Indiana House of Representatives. The upper floor was split into two rooms, one for the Indiana State Senate and another for the Indiana Supreme Court. In 1825, the capital was moved to Indianapolis and the building was given to Harrison County to be used as a courthouse.

George Rogers Clark Monument

425 S. 2nd St.
Vincennes, IN 47591
38.67828903498854, -87.53561696442749

A massive Greek style stone monument stands along the Wabash River in the city of Vincennes. It stands on what is believed to be the location of the British fort of Sackville. The monument is dedicated to George Rogers Clark whose forces captured Fort Sackville in 1779 during the northwest campaign of the Revolutionary War.

After the war, Clark was given a large tract of land along the Ohio River in the Indiana Territory. He financed much of his wartime efforts with his own money, and due to poor recordkeeping on either Clark's or the government's part, he was not reimbursed for the money he had borrowed. For the remainder of his life, he was hounded by creditors and did not have the resources to develop the land he was given. He built a small log cabin along the Ohio River. Near his cabin along the river, he met up with his younger brother William Clark of the famed Lewis and Clark Expedition to explore the land in the Louisiana Purchase. He lived in the cabin until he had a stroke and was badly burned in an accident and lost one of his legs. He moved to Kentucky and lived with his sister where he died in 1818.

In 1929, local residents wanted to commemorate the 150th anniversary of Clark's campaign. The state of Indiana chose to build a memorial to General Clark's triumph in the 1930s. With help from the United States government, $2.5 million was raised, and the monument was dedicated on June 14, 1936, by President Franklin Roosevelt. It is considered the largest memorial of its type east of Washington D.C.

A replica of Clark's original cabin was constructed near the Falls of the Ohio where the first one once stood. Tragically, it was destroyed by an arsonist's fire in 2019.

USS LST-325

US Navel Archives

610 NW Riverside Dr.
Evansville, IN 47708
37.97315462375895, -87.58018270670269

An old World War II ship is tied up to a dock on the Ohio
River in Evansville, Indiana. It is no ordinary ship and has
large metal doors on the bow of the massive gray ship. Painted
on the side is the number 325. The ship is a Landing Tank Ship

(LST). Unlike some of the Navy's larger ships such as Aircraft Carriers and Destroyers, smaller vessels were just given a number rather than a name. LST-325 was launched in October 1942. The old ship may only be known by its number, but that does not mean it wasn't important to the war effort.

LSTs were designed to carry tanks, trucks and supplies across the ocean. They were unique because they had a flat bottom so they could sail up to the shore and offload cargo through the front doors. They did not need a dock and were used in amphibious assaults.

On the D-Day invasion of June 6, 1944, LST-325 carried 59 vehicles, 30 officers and a total of 396 enlisted men on its first trip. Over the next nine months, LST-325 made more than forty trips across the English Channel, carrying thousands of men and equipment needed by troops to successfully liberate Europe. At the end of the war, LST-325 was decommissioned. Unlike most of the landing ships, it was not scrapped and got a second life; being sent to Greece in September 1964, she served in the Hellenic Navy as RHS Syros as part of the grant-in-aid program from 1964 to 1999.

In 2000, the old ship was purchased by a group of retired military men who formed The USS LST Memorial, Inc. The historic ship sailed across the ocean and up the Mississippi and Ohio Rivers to its home port of Evansville. It is the last navigable complete LST ship in operation.

The ship ended up in Evansville because during World War II, the riverfront in Evansville had a shipyard that built LSTs. At its peak, the Evansville Shipyard employed a workforce of over 19,000 and completed two ships per week, becoming the largest inland producer of LSTs in the U.S. The shipyard was originally contracted to build twenty-four ships, but the city would eventually produce 167 LSTs and 35 other vessels. Moored to a dock in Evansville, LST-325 floats as a reminder of the city's war efforts and honors all those that served on the mighty LSTs.

Located in Crane, Indiana is Naval Support Activity Crane that includes over 3,000 buildings and more than 98 square miles. The base, named in honor of Commodore William Montgomery Crane, is the third largest naval installation in the world by geographic area and employs over three thousand people.

Chapter 2
Central Indiana

The Log Cabin Chapel

1 Providence Pl.
St Mary-Of-The-Woods, IN 47876
39.50991258755498, -87.46089691741115

Saint Mary-of-the-Woods College is located a few miles northwest of Terre Haute. It is the oldest college in Indiana. In 1839, the first bishop of the Diocese of Vincennes in Indiana requested help from his home country of France. He asked for a congregation to assist in teaching the early pioneers of Indiana. Mother Theodore Guerin was asked to take on the challenge. Reluctant at first, she agreed to lead five other Sisters of Providence to Indiana. After two months of sailing across the Atlantic Ocean and traveling into the heart of America, they made it to the forests of Indiana. The six sisters founded an academy in Saint Mary-of-the-Woods for the education of young women. In 1846, Saint Mary-of-the-Woods College was granted the first charter for the higher education of women in the state of Indiana. It was the first women's college to offer journalism courses and a degree in secondary education for women.

The beautiful campus is home to several historic and religious structures and buildings. Nestled among the trees and green lawns is a log cabin. It is a replica of a cabin the sisters used as a chapel when they first completed their long journey to Indiana. Logs to construct the replica were donated from a cabin in southern Indiana owned by David and Faye Masterson of Owensville. Construction of the log chapel was done by inmates of the U.S. Federal Penitentiary in Terre Haute.

In 2015, Saint Mary-of-the-Woods College Board of Trustees voted unanimously to become fully coeducational and now educates both men and women.

The National Road

Near Art Nehf Field
Rose Hulman University
5500 Wabash Ave.
Terre Haute, IN 47803
39.47969876657941, -87.33178682091467

This cute little stone English cottage style building stands on the campus of Rose-Hulman Institute of Technology. It is used as a concession stand for the soccer and baseball fields, but it was originally a service station in Terre Haute before being moved to the college in 1999. The old gas station was originally built in 1931 and serviced cars traveling along the National Road.

The road was built long before the invention of the automobile and was the first federally funded road in the United States. Early politicians debated on the role the U.S. Government would take in the building of the nation. Some wanted the government to fund infrastructure projects, while others wanted private entities to pay for and control things such as roads and bridges and pay for them with tolls.

In 1806, Congress authorized the construction of the Cumberland Road between the Potomac and Ohio Rivers. It replaced the wagon and footpaths and was paved with gravel. To promote expansion into the northwest territory, the road was extended to St. Louis Missouri and funded by the sale of land in Ohio. The road passed through the Indiana towns of Indianapolis and Terre Haute. In 1927, when numbered routes were designated, the many parts of the National Road became US-40. It is along this route east of Terre Haute where you will see the little stone cottage service station next to Rose-Hulman's ball fields.

Interstate 70 parallels US-40 and provided motorists with a faster route when it was constructed in Indiana in the 1960s.

Bridgeton

8104 Bridgeton Rd.
Bridgeton, IN 47836
39.64969764054094, -87.17617103731091

Bridgeton is situated in a rural area of Indiana between Rockville and Brazil, Indiana. The picturesque historic town draws visitors to its historic buildings and quaint shops. The town got its start in the 1820s when a mill was built on the bank of the Big Racoon Creek. Originally, the town was known as Lockwood Mills for the local mill, but it later became known as Sodom because of the drinking and fighting that took place. In 1849, when a post office was established it was given the name of Bridgeton.

To aid the farmers in crossing the creek, a wooden covered bridge was constructed in 1868. It replaced two previous smaller bridges. The covered bridge carried traffic for almost a century before a new modern bridge was built beside it. In 2005, the historic and beloved bridge was destroyed by a fire set by the hands of an arsonist. A historically accurate bridge was constructed the following year and is open to pedestrians.

The little town is a wonderful place to visit to get away from the hustle and bustle of the big city and be reminded of a simpler time in the Hoosier State. The historic mill still grinds grain to this day and is the oldest continuously operating mill west of the Allegheny Mountains. The town hosts several events throughout the year; its most popular is the Covered Bridge Festival in October.

The oldest building in Bridgeton is the Masonic Lodge. It is one of the last Masonic Moon lodges in the United States. Meetings were held on the night of a full moon because of poor roads and traveling conditions to make travel safer and easier by the light of a bright moon.

The Grave in the Middle of the Road

East of Sugar Creek on E. 400 S.
Franklin, IN 46131
39.41989978264244, -85.97592936955161

County Road 400 travels east and west near Franklin, Indiana. Just east of where it crosses the Sugar Creek is a concrete median with a marker surrounded by coins and flowers. The marker denotes the gravesite of Nancy Kerlin Barnett. She died in 1831 and was buried on a hill overlooking the creek.

In 1912, it was decided to run a new road through the cemetery, and the bodies were to be moved to a new graveyard. When construction of the new road began, Nancy's grandson Daniel G. Doty protected her grave with a shotgun, claiming it was her wish to be buried where she was. As the story goes, he remained there as workers moved the bodies and routed the road around her grave. The headstone and eventually a historical marker remained in the center of the road for decades.

In 2016, the road needed to be repaired, and it was decided that Nancy's grave was a hazard to motorists and farm equipment. Plans were made to have her remains exhumed and replaced after the road construction was completed. To everyone's surprise, the University of Indiana team exhumed the remains and found six more people's skeletons in the grave. The bodies of two women, a man and four children were dug up. It is believed the body of the man had been previously dug up and placed back in the grave. Exactly who the bodies belong to are unknown, but it is assumed one is that of Nancy Barnett. It also makes one ponder if Daniel Doty did not want the grave disturbed because it would expose a secret he did not want revealed.

After the section of County Road 400 had been repaved with a new median, the remains of all seven bodies were buried under the median, and a new marker for Nancy was placed on top of it. The gravesite still remains in the middle of the road and is one of the United State's most unique gravesites.

The Tower Tree

150 Courthouse Square
Greensburg, IN 47240
39.33699238720317, -85.48348597915678

Indiana has several historic and beautiful county courthouses. The old courthouse in Greensburg is notable not only for its architecture, but also the tree growing out of the top of its tower.

The current Decatur County Courthouse was completed in 1861. About ten years later, people began noticing some

branches sticking out of the roof on the tower. Five different trees appeared to be growing on the roof of the courthouse tower. In the 1880s, a worker was sent up to the top of the tower for fear of damage to the building. Three of the trees were removed, leaving a pair to continue growing. One of the trees died and is now on display at the County Historical Society.

The tower continues to have a tree growing out of the roof. Workers recently went up to the roof to check on the tree and trim back some of its branches. After being tested by Purdue University, the species was identified as mulberry. No one knows how seeds got up to the roof or how a tree has managed to survive for so long in such a strange environment, but people from all around stop in Greensburg to marvel at the tower tree.

The tree was featured on an episode on the television show *Ripley's Believe It or Not.*

Duck Creek Aqueduct

 19001 Pennington Rd,
Metamora, IN 47030
39.446226861035946, -85.12999792347141

Before railroads, canals were a vital source of transportation. The Whitewater Canal in Southeastern Indiana allowed boats to travel 76 miles from the Ohio River to Hagerstown, Indiana. The canal was built in 1846, but over time, it became unnecessary as railroad tracks and roads replaced it. Most of the canal is gone, but one of the most interesting components still stands today near the town of Metamora.

A wooden aqueduct crosses over the Duck Creek, making it the only remaining covered wooden aqueduct in the United States. A "water bridge" used to carry canal boats over the creek. It was constructed in 1846 as part of the original canal. Oak timbers created a trough to carry the water across the aqueduct. It was strengthened in 1868 and repaired in 1901. After abandonment and deterioration, the Duck Creek Aqueduct was restored to its present appearance in 1949.

Although boats no longer used the canal, the water from it was used to power mills such as the historic mill in Metamora. In 1946, the State of Indiana purchased a 14-mile section of the Whitewater Canal, including the mill, as a state historic site. The town has several small shops and is a wonderful place to visit for history buffs.

A few miles southeast of Metamora along Highway 52 is an old lock that was part of the Whitewater Canal.

Hoosier Hill

 11960 Elliott Rd.
Lynn, IN 47355
40.0013604429029, -84.84868359314362

In the farmland on the eastern side of the state is Indiana's

highest point. About twenty miles north of Richmond, Indiana

is Hoosier Hill at 1257 feet. It seems more like a bump than a

hill surrounded by rolling farmland. It sits on private property but is open to the public. A boulder marks the spot, and a mailbox holds a logbook for visitors to sign. It is not the most impressive high point of the fifty states, but it is a spot to check off your list and say you have been there.

A.H. Marshall was the first person to successfully make it to each U.S. state high point after standing on top of Hoosier Hill in 1936.

Union Literary Institute

8605 E 600 S.
Union City, IN 47390
40.07748714168061, -84.81639143557327

A dilapidated old brick building surrounded by farmland stands near the Indiana-Ohio border between Winchester, Indiana and Greenville, Ohio. It is in terrible shape and on the brink of collapse after being converted into a barn, but it is one of the most historically significant buildings in the Hoosier State. It was built in 1846 as the Union Literary

Institute. Literary institute is what they called schools that were not affiliated with a religious group "literary institutes".

Union Literary Institute was one of the first schools to offer higher education without regard to color or sex before the Civil War. It was also the first school in Indiana to allow both black and white students to learn together. The school was a manual labor school that allowed students to work four hours per day to cover the cost of their education. The school closed in 1924, and it was sold. The building's second floor was removed, and it was converted into a barn. In 2008, the building was donated to the Union Literary Institute Preservation Society, which is trying to stabilize the building so that people can see what remains. A historical marker was placed near the building in 2016 to tell some of the structure's remarkable story.

Notable attendees included Hiram Revels, the first black U.S. Senator, and James S. Hinton, the first black person elected to the Indiana House of Representatives.

Randolph County Infirmary

1882 US 27 South
Winchester, IN 47394
40.13748986157614, -84.96598700377263

South of Winchester along US-27 is a large brick building.
Above the front door carved in stone are the words
RANDOLPH CO. INFIRMARY. It was built in 1899 and
served the citizens of Randolph County for over a century.
The property started as the county poor farm in 1851, taking

care of the mentally and physically disabled, elderly and orphans. The large 5000 square foot building that stands today cared for many people over the decades. It has also seen its share of tragedy. It is believed that over two hundred people have died in the facility, many from tuberculosis and some to suicide and possibly murder. It is said that one man died after being pushed out a second story window.

The infirmary contained up to 350 acres for farming and livestock, and it also has a cemetery with unmarked graves for the people who died under its care. In the 1990s, it was used as a nursing home; it closed in 2008. The current owner, Dann Allen, purchased the historic old asylum in 2016 to save it from demolition. It is currently being used as a paranormal attraction for visitors to explore paranormal activity. You can learn more tours at their website

www.hauntedrandolphcounty.com

According to *The Indianapolis News* from 1918, "The Mummy Mose" was buried in the infirmary cemetery. In the early 1900s, it had been on exhibition at fairs in western Ohio and eastern Indiana. It was the body of a tramp found murdered in a barn near Lima that no one claimed. A local undertaker embalmed and preserved it, but the body began to show signs of decay, and it was ordered to be buried at the county-owned cemetery.

Holliday Park Ruins

6363 Spring Mill Rd.
Indianapolis, IN 46260
39.87071283212709, -86.16326667935935

Holliday Park sits about five miles north of Indianapolis, and it is where you will find ruins of a long forgotten building. The strange thing is they are not remnants of an Indiana building but one that stood on Broadway Street in New York City. The twenty-six story St. Paul building was one of the tallest buildings in New York when it was constructed in 1898. By the 1950s, it had become outdated and slated for demolition to make way for a new skyscraper. Above the entrance to the historic building were three sculptures created by Austrian artist Carl Bitter.

At the time of demolition, they were estimated to be worth $150,000. They were titled "The Races of Man", which depicted three men—one Caucasian, one African-American and one Asian—supporting the base of the building. Several people and organizations came forward asking for the sculptures to save them from the landfill. Western Electric, which owned the building, requested proposals of final displays of the statutes. It was artist Elmer Taflinger's concept for an installation he called "The Ruins" that won over Western Electric, and they donated the sculptures to Indianapolis.

Years went by as Taflinger gathered other architectural details and components from Indianapolis buildings that were demolished. He obtained 26 Greek columns salvaged from the Sisters of the Good Shepherd Convent and four statues of goddesses that had stood above the entrance to the Marion County Courthouse before it was demolished.

Working for years on the project, the mayor became concerned in 1970 that the sculptures would be returned back to New York. The project was ordered completed and dedicated in 1973. The art installation stood for years but over time fell into disrepair and truly became ruins. The reflecting pool leaked and all the water was drained. The gardens and landscaping became overgrown, and the bricks were falling out, making it dangerous. By 2013, the Ruins were fenced off and threatened with demolition. The nonprofit Friends of Holliday Park raised $3.2 million and were able to renovate the art installation, making it a beautiful attraction for visitors to admire.

The Rotary Jail

225 N Washington St.
Crawfordsville, IN 47933
40.043848058646965, -86.901600885056

Crawfordsville is about fifty miles northwest of Indianapolis. Because it needed a new jail in the late 1800s and is close to Indiana's largest city, it has one of the most unique jails in the country. Architect William H. Brown patented the rotary jail in

1881, and it was built by Haugh, Ketcham & Co. iron foundry in Indianapolis.

Crawfordsville built its new jail using the innovative rotary jail system. It consisted of a large round metal "carousel" divided into eight wedge shaped sections. The exterior had bars around it except for one door. A guard could crank a handle and the cells would rotate to the door, minimizing the chances of escape and the need for several guards. It worked in theory, but after approximately fifteen rotary jails were built in the midwest, the design flaws became apparent.

In the event of a fire, the inmates were trapped unless a guard was willing to risk being killed in the fire to crank the handle to rotate the jail. Even more problematic was the chances of a limb being broken or amputated in the bars as cells rotated. This was a problem that happened when intoxicated people passed out against the bars out of view from the guard rotating the cells. By the 1930s, all the rotary jails had either been dismantled or welded in place and new doors added for each cell.

The Crawfordsville rotary jail was welded up in the 1930s and continued to house prisoners until 1973. No longer used as a jail, the building was purchased by Montgomery County Cultural Foundation and was converted into a museum. The old rotary mechanism was repaired, and it is the only fully functioning rotary jail.

The center of the jail allowed for plumbing and each cell had a toilet. It was rare at the time, especially since many homes did not even have indoor plumbing.

LORAN Station

 1534 W County Rd 200 S.
Dana, IN 47847
39.853562967853385, -87.4914986343788

In the modern era of GPS navigation, anyone with a smartphone can easily pinpoint their location. Before satellites orbited the earth, it was much more difficult for someone to figure out their location. For generations, sailors used a compass and stars to navigate. During World War II, a long range navigation system or LORAN was developed. It consisted of a series of radio stations that emitted a signal for electronic instrumentation on ships and airplanes to triangulate their position.

After the war, the Coast Guard took over the LORAN system, and it was implemented on many commercial ships. The Great Lakes is one of the busiest waterways in the world, and in 1967, to aid in navigation, a LORAN station was set up near Dana, Indiana. With GPS satellites sent into orbit in the 80s, the LORAN system became unnecessary, and the station in Indiana ceased operating in 2010. I find it interesting that ships navigating the Great Lakes depended on a station hundreds of miles away in Indiana surrounded by corn fields and dairy farms. Remains of the station and the antenna can still be seen from the road that passes by it.

While doing research for the LORAN station, I noticed what looked like an old military base about three miles to the east. I found out it was the Newport Chemical Depot, previously known as the Wabash River Ordnance Works. It started out making high explosives and then VX nerve agent used in chemical warfare. The site was shut down in 2008, and the VX agent was neutralized. It is now a private industrial park. It is amazing and terrifying the things a person learns when exploring the backroads.

Roads Hotel

 150 E Main St.
Atlanta, IN 46031
40.21602319273977, -86.02536975477689

The town of Atlanta is located between Indianapolis and Kokomo. An old wooden two-story building sits on Main Street. Flanked by two large trees, it was built in 1893, and ran as a hotel by Newton Roads and his family. The town was a popular stop for trains traveling the nearby tracks. Many guests have stayed in the hotel, including outlaws such as Al Capone and John Dillanger. During Prohibition, it operated as a speakeasy and brothel.

The Roads Hotel has also seen its share of tragedy. Newton's son Everett was diagnosed with tuberculosis at age nineteen, and he was confined to isolation in the hotel until he died. Newton and his wife Clara also died in the hotel. A few guests have died in the old hotel, including some who committed suicide while staying there. Because of its turbulent history, it is considered one of the most haunted places in Indiana. Visitors have claimed to see apparitions of men, women and children. They have witnessed strange occurrences such as disembodied voices, hearing footsteps, lights turning on and off, and doors opening and closing on their own. The old hotel is decorated to look as if it did a century ago, and the owners welcome people to experience it for themselves. You can find out more on their website www.roadshotel.com.

The town was originally named Buena Vista. Because there was already a town of the same name, it was renamed Atlanta in1885. Some believed the new name was influenced by the men who returned home from the Civil War and named after the city in Georgia.

James Dean

200 N Main St.
Fairmount, IN 46928
40.417280693232485,-85.65018584506062

Hollywood has had several male actors who are the epitome of cool, but one name that rises to the top is James Dean. What most people don't know is that he was born in the small Indiana town of Marion. At the age of six, he moved with his family to California and after his mother's death when he was nine, his father sent him back to Fairmount, Indiana. He lived with his aunt and uncle on their farm while his father served during World War II.

Dean was an exceptional and popular student. He played on the varsity baseball and basketball teams, studied drama, and competed in public speaking through the Indiana High School Forensic Association. After graduating from Fairmount High School in May 1949, he moved back to California with his dog Max to live with his father and stepmother. He enrolled in UCLA to study law, but to his father's disappointment, he switched to drama. I think drama worked out rather well for him.

He also loved cars and took to racing them. He competed in a few races until Warner Brothers prohibited him from racing while filming the movie Giant. After filming ended, Dean purchased a new 1955 Porsche 550 Spyder and entered the upcoming Salinas Road Race. On September 30, 1955, his life was cut short at the age of 27 when he died in an accident while driving his new Porsche to the race in Salinas. James Dean Memorial Park was created in his hometown of Fairmount, where a bust of the famous actor can be seen. The town also has a James Dean museum and several sites dedicated to the late actor.

Every year on the last full weekend in September, Fairmount holds the James Dean Festival.

Old State House Quarry

250 McCormick Creek Park Rd.
Spencer, IN 47460
39.29511175527012, -86.73233690492351

If Indiana was not nicknamed the Hoosier State, it might have been called the Limestone State since it was used in constructing so many of the United States most famous buildings. Some of them include: The Pentagon, Lincoln Memorial, Empire State Building, Grand Central Station, and many state capitals.

While most quarries are off limits to the public, there is one historic quarry in McCormick Creek State Park that is accessible to the public. It was used to build the old State House. Limestone was first cut from it in 1878 because the limestone outcropping was easily accessible. When a railroad bridge was washed out in 1880, it was never rebuilt and because there was better quality limestone to be found nearby, mining at the site ended.

If you take trail number 2 past the CCC Recreation Building-Nature Museum, it will lead you down to the old quarry. It is amazing to see the large limestone ledges covered in moss and plants. It is like looking at old ancient ruins in the jungle. If you climb up on some of the ledges, you can still see the holes and tool markings from the workers when the quarry was abandoned after the railroad bridge was washed out. It is about a mile hike down to the quarry. The trail is downhill all the way, so that means it is uphill all the way back. It was not too difficult, but I took my time getting back. I recommend taking some water if you do the hike in the summer on a hot day.

McCormick Creek State Park is also home to the Historic Peden Farm Site, which can be seen along trail number 9.

Ten O'Clock Line

5471, IN-67.
Gosport, IN 47433
39.354856630495576, -86.66767435122989

Indiana Route 67 passes by the town of Gosport, and near the road in a small park is a stone marker with frontiersmen and native Americans images carved into it. A historical marker stands next to it that marks the Ten O'Clock Line. Future president and Indiana Territory Governor William Henry Harrison negotiated several treaties with the tribes in the northwest territory.

In 1809, the Treaty of Fort Wayne was signed by the Potawatomi, Delaware, Eel Rivers, and Miami tribes. To mark the boundary line, a spear was driven into the ground, and its shadow cast the line established by the treaty. The line runs at an angle across southern Indiana and became known as the Ten O'Clock Line. The historic town of Gosport is the only town directly on the line.

The Jail and the Cult Leader

802 Conner St.
Noblesville, IN 46060
40.04583842176356, -86.01443913452928

The historic and beautiful Hamilton County Courthouse
stands in downtown Noblesville northeast of Indianapolis.
Next to the courthouse is a brick Queen Anne style house with
a large addition on the rear. It served as the sheriff's residence,
and the jail was attached to the back of it. At the time it was

constructed in 1877, it was common for the local sheriff to live next to the jail and his wife and family were expected to feed the prisoners and maintain the jail.

At one time, there was a tunnel that ran to the courthouse to transfer inmates to trials. The tunnel has been filled, and the jail was closed in the 1970s. It was leased to the Hamilton County Historical Society and is now used as a museum. Visitors can learn about the county's history and see what the jail was like a century ago and where one of the most notorious and evil persons was held as a teenager.

Charles Manson was born in 1937 in Cincinnati, Ohio. His mother had a rough and turbulent life when Charles was young, and she was constantly in trouble with the law. Around the age of twelve, he and his mother moved to Indianapolis. Charles began getting in trouble for petty theft and ditching school. In 1949, at the age of 13, he was placed in the Gibault School for Boys in Terre Haute. Ran by Catholic priests, it was a strict school where punishment for even the smallest infraction included beatings with either a wooden paddle or a leather strap. Manson ran away from Gibault and slept in the woods, under bridges, and wherever else he could find shelter.

He continued his life of crime, committing armed robbery and stealing cars. He was sent to the Indiana Boys School in Plainfield southwest of Indianapolis. He was repeatedly beaten and abused by the other "students" and escaped eighteen times. During one of his escapes, he was apprehended and lodged in the Hamilton County Jail in Noblesville. Eventually, he moved on to California, and as they say, "the rest is history".

In 1925, head of the Indiana Ku Klux Klan, D.C. Stephenson was held at the jail for second-degree murder, and his trial took place at the Hamilton County Courthouse. Because of the publicity, his trial was moved from Indianapolis to Nobelsville.

The House of Happy Little Trees

620 W Minnetrista Blvd.
Muncie, IN 47303
40.202648052108536,-85.39267135435801

Bob Ross is known for painting "happy little trees" in his landscape paintings of mountains on his television series The Joy Of Painting, which aired on PBS. What most people don't know is that many of his paintings were created in an historic mansion in Indiana.

His first season was recorded in 1983 at a PBS station in Virginia. Afterwards, he traveled the country giving classes in various cities. One of those cities was Muncie, Indiana. The local PBS station WIPB was so mesmerized by his skill and calm demeanor that they offered him the chance to record his TV show in their studio. It was not your typical studio. It was the former home of Lucius L. Ball, who came to Muncie with his brothers to produce mason jars.

The home eventually became the studio of PBS affiliate WIPB. Bob Ross lived in Florida but came up to Muncie to record his TV show. Black cloth backdrops were hung in a room on the first floor. He set up his easel and painted while a cameraman recorded it. When he cleaned his brush by dipping it in turpentine and then dried it by "beating the devil out of it" on his easel's leg, it splattered everywhere in the small room. That is why he joked and laughed many times while cleaning his brush.

He recorded fifteen seasons in the mansion until they moved to a new state of the art studio on the campus of Ball

University. Bob Ross died in 1995 from Lymphoma, but his TV show continues on in syndication and on the internet. The mansion is still used as offices for WIPB, but they have recently opened it up to visitors to see Ross's original studio. You can learn more at their website

https://www.minnetrista.net/bobrossexperience.

Lucius L. Ball's home and his brothers' mansions along the White River came to be known as Minnetrista, derived from the Sioux word meaning "a gathering place by the water". The Minnetrista Cultural Center is down the road from the Ball brother's mansions. It is a beautiful neighborhood to drive through and marvel at the historic homes.

Chapter 3
Northern Indiana

Tippecanoe

200 Battleground Ave.
West Lafayette, IN 47906
40.50623732330649, -86.84466686443231

I don't remember a lot from my history classes in grade school, but for some reason the saying "Tippecanoe and Tyler Too" stuck in my brain. I had to stop at the Tippecanoe battlefield north of Laffayette and learn a little history and why the things I was taught in school were important. An 85-foot tall obelisk was erected at the site of the battlefield in 1908 to memorialize the importance of the battle that took place on November 7, 1811.

The leader of the Shawnee, Tecumseh, opposed the 1809 Treaty of Fort Wayne, which other tribal chiefs had agreed to, and vowed to fight for their land. Tecumseh and his brother Tenskwatawa were in the settlement of Prophetstown on the Wabash River where the Tippecanoe River flows into it. A force of one thousand men led by William Henry Harrison set up camp near the Tippecanoe River. Tecumseh left Prophetstown in search of more warriors from other tribes and help from the British Allies. He told his brother not to attack until he returned.

Tenskwatawa disobeyed his brother's order and led a sneak attack of the camp in the early morning hours. The American forces were able to fend off the attack after two hours of battle. As the Native American warriors retreated, the Americans on horseback rode to Prophetstown and burned down the village. It was a major turning point in the battle between the new country and the Native Americans. The battle garnered great recognition for Harrison, and he was known as "Old Tippecanoe". When John Tyler became his running mate, they adopted the slogan "Tippecanoe and Tyler Too".

A number of counties in Indiana were named for American soldiers at the battle: Bartholomew, Daveiss, Spencer, Tipton and Warrick.

Old Ben and the Stump

"SYCAMORE STUMP"

1402 Defenbaugh St.
Kokomo, IN 46902
40.46921347028825, -86.14389798413134

Highland Park is located to the south of downtown Kokomo. There you will find a visitors center with rooms on either side surrounded with windows. They are not there for people to look out of but rather for people to peer through to view what is inside. The building holds two of Indiana's largest treasures.

One is a large sycamore stump. The tree stood a few miles west of Kokomo and is said to be over one hundred feet tall and over 1500 years old. The enormous tree came down in a storm in the early 1900s. Enthralled by the size of the stump, in 1916, Jacob Bergman, commissioner of Kokomo's city park, paid a farmer to haul the massive stump to the park with his tractor. The stump was 57 feet around, 18 feet wide and 12 feet tall, and Bergman had plans to cut a doorway in it and build a staircase in the hollow stump to a viewing platform on top. His plans never materialized ,and the stump sat outside for years. In 1938, the National Youth Administration built an open air shelter around the stump. In 1989, it was enclosed as part of a new pavilion with another of Kokomo's prized

possessions.

Old Ben, the World's Largest Steer, was large from the time it was born in 1902. Weighing almost 125 pounds at birth, he grew to weigh about 4500 pounds, well above the average weight for most steers, which is about 1200 pounds. The owners, who lived about ten miles north of Kokomo, had several offers to purchase him for circuses and sideshows, but they kept him for themselves. They traveled to many Indiana fairs and showed him to the public in his own private tent.

At his death in 1910, he was 16 feet long from nose to tail. After his death, Old Ben was stuffed and mounted on a base with wheels. He was either donated or sold to the city of Kokomo. They kept him in storage and put him on display at times for the public to marvel at how large he is. After the building was completed in 1989, he was put on permanent display opposite the sycamore stump.

> The city was named after the Miami Indian leader Chief Kokomo.

Seiberling Mansion

 1200 W Sycamore St.
Kokomo, IN 46901
40.486899337956, -86.14419296990292

Kokomo, Indiana's Old Silk Stocking Neighborhood, named

for the hosiery worn by those who could afford it in the late

1800s, has a number of old historic houses, but there is one mansion that stands out among them. The magnificent home was built in 1889 by Monroe Seiberling, who was the owner of the Diamond Plate Glass Company. The Romanesque Revival-Queen Ann style mansion has 27 rooms and 10 fireplaces.

After World War II, Indiana University purchased the home and used it as part of their campus. By 1964, the university no longer used the old house, and it sat empty and in a state of disrepair. After talk of demolition, the Howard County Historical Society purchased the home in 1972. After extensive renovation, the home is now used as a museum.

Gene Stratton Porter and Limberlost

200 6th St.
Geneva, IN 46740
40.589674281649586, -84.95991389980871

US-27 takes motorists along the eastern side of Indiana and passes through the town of Geneva. Named for the town in Switzerland, there you will see a large log cabin style house that looks like a lodge in a National Park. It was the home of author Gene Stratton Porter.

Born on a farm in Lagro, Indiana in 1863, she was the youngest of twelve children in the Stratton family. She spent much of her youth exploring the farm, studying birds and nature. At the age of twenty, she met Charles Porter, who she married about two years later. Porter was thirteen years older than Gene, and a successful businessman. He was a druggist and owned a few drug stores in eastern Indiana, including Geneva. Gene and Charles moved to Geneva and built a log home in 1895. Designed by Gene Stratton-Porter, the rustic Queen Anne two-story log cabin style home was made from Wisconsin white cedar. It has fourteen rooms, a wrap-around porch and a conservatory where Gene grew several plants.

While Charles was busy tending to his business affairs, Gene grew restless staying at home. She spent her time exploring the nearby Limberlost Swamp. It was the name of the swamp that inspired the name of her log home. The swamp got its name from a man named Limber Jim, who got lost while hunting in the swamp. When the news spread, the cry went out "Limber's lost!"

During her time at Geneva and the swamp, Gene wrote several books. Two of her most popular novels were *Freckles* and *A Girl of the Limberlost*. She also learned photography and photographed the swamp and documented its surroundings publishing nature books. When asked by someone at Kodak how she managed to create such stunning prints, she did not want to admit that her bathroom was the darkroom and she developed prints on turkey platters. By 1913, the swamp she loved was mostly drained, and she and Charles built a new log home on the shores of Sylvan Lake, which she named Cabin at Wildflower Woods. Stratton-Porter wrote twenty-six books, including twelve novels, eight nature studies, two books of poetry, and four collections of stories and children's books which collectively sold over one million copies. She moved to California in 1918, where she died in an automobile accident in 1924 at the age of 61.

Both of her homes, Limberlost and Cabin at Wildflower Woods, each operate as state historic sites and welcome visitors to explore the life of an incredible woman from Indiana.

The Resting Place of
Johnny Appleseed

3800 Parnell Ave.
Fort Wayne, IN 46805
41.11181918011566, -85.12314460276602

Growing up in the midwest, I remember the tall tales of colorful people such as Paul Bunyan, John Henry and Johnny Appleseed. I am not sure if all of them are based on real people, but Johnny Appleseed was the nickname of a real person. Born in Massachusetts in 1774, John Chapman moved to western Pennsylvania when he was a teenager. A few years later, his father and his siblings moved to the Ohio Territory, where Chapman worked on his father's farm. He started an apprenticeship at a nearby apple orchard that began his journey of growing apple trees.

Chapman traveled around the region, helping people plant and grow apple trees. They were not the apples that most people are familiar with today. They were smaller bitter sour apples used in the making of hard cider. Because of the lack of fresh water, hard cider was safer to drink and was less likely to contain bacteria and diseases. The fact that a person could get drunk from it also helped in its popularity. Having apples to make cider was more of a necessity to survive the harsh conditions of the unsettled midwest. John Chapman was well liked for his kindness and generosity, giving out seeds and helping people plant them. He acquired the nickname of Johnny Appleseed as he traveled around from homestead to homestead.

Chapman traveled throughout the midwest during his lifetime. In 1834, he came to the Fort Wayne area and purchased land along the Maumee River for a nursery. While he was visiting a friend in Fort Wayne, he became ill and died in 1845. The exact date of his death is not certain, and a stone that is believed to mark his grave is located in a small park near the Allen County War Memorial Coliseum. Up on a small hill with two apple trees and a wrought iron fence is a memorial where people leave apples in his memory. The Johnny Appleseed Festival is held at the park every year on the third weekend in September.

> The driveway to the park off Parnell Avenue can be a little tricky to find. It is next to the power lines and has a small sign for Johnny Appleseed.

Kingsbury Ordnance Plant

Kingsbury Fish & Wildlife Area
5344 S. Hupp Rd.
La Porte, IN 46350
41.519965637012355, -86.62439014958976

The Kingsbury Fish and Wildlife Area is located between South Bend and Valparaiso. Driving through it, you will notice concrete bunkers and strange signs warning of unexploded ordnance shells. That is because at one time it was the Kingsbury Ordnance Plant.

120

During World War II, the government needed a facility to manufacture munitions for the war effort. They chose northern Indiana for its remote location and access to water and transportation. I can attest to it being remote. It is a long drive through rural farmland to get to the wildlife area. The military wanted it away from any large population in case of a disastrous accidental explosion. The property covered twenty square miles, and bunkers and buildings were spread out so that if an explosion happened in one building, it would not ignite another one.

The plant needed nearly twenty thousand workers. The closest town of La Porte only had a population of about sixteen thousand at the time. The plant recruited employees from all over northern Indiana and southern Michigan. To house the workers, the town of Kingsford Heights was built by the plant officials. Because of the large number of men who served in the military during the war, half of the plant's workforce were women.

The plant operated until the end of the war then briefly opened for the Korean War. It was officially shut down in 1960 and five years later converted into a wildlife refuge. It is strange driving around the massive site and seeing the remnants of the factory. The larger buildings are now part of an industrial park. If you go exploring the area, be sure to obey all posted signs.

Indiana also had an army ammunition plant along the Ohio River near Louisville. It is now part of the Charlestown State Park. I asked the ranger if any of the former buildings were accessible, and they informed me they are inaccessible to the public.

The President's Funeral Train

103 N Illinois St.
Wanatah, IN 46390
41.430118232753436, -86.90029511550591

The small town of Wanatah is located in the farmland of northwestern Indiana. Behind the grain elevator is a small park. In it is a red wooden caboose that has been restored by the historical society and has historic memorabilia and artifacts on display. Near the caboose is a sign that stands as a reminder of one of the darkest days in the history of the United States.

After President Lincoln's assassination in April of 1865, a funeral trail transported his body back to his home in Springfield, Illinois. The train left Washington DC and followed his campaign route, traveling up through New York and then down to Ohio and over to Indianapolis. From there, it traveled up to Michigan City on its way to Chicago.

Mourners gathered along the tracks to view the passing train. They came for miles by wagons, horseback or even walking dirt roads to get a glimpse of the train and the railroad car that carried the slain president. It is believed over one and a half million people came to view the train at a time when the entire population of the United States was thirty million. The funeral train passed through the town of Wanatah on its route to Springfield.

The funeral train also carried the body of Lincoln's son, Willie, who had died from typhoid fever three years earlier at the age of eleven. Willie's casket had been held in a vault in a Georgetown cemetery awaiting interment in Springfield at the end of Lincoln's presidency.

The Old Sheriff's House and Jail

226 S Main St.
Crown Point, IN 46307
41.41570052119493, -87.36397054975147

The town of Crown Point is about ten miles south of Gary. A block south of the historic courthouse at the center of town is the old jail and sheriff's house. It was built in 1882, and at the time of its construction it was considered to be one of the Hoosier State's best jails. It held many inmates over the years, and it was in use until it closed in 1974. It held one of the most notorious gangsters, at least for a short time, until he escaped.

In 1934, John Dillinger was captured in Tucson, Arizona and extradited back to Indiana. He was facing charges for the murder of a policeman who was killed during a Dillinger gang bank robbery in East Chicago, Indiana. He was held in the Crown Point Jail. Local policemen bragged about the jail and believed it to be escape-proof.

In March 1935, Dillenger surprised the guards with a gun during morning exercise. He escaped with fifteen other inmates. After his escape, he stole the police chief's car to make his getaway. It is still unclear as to whether he carved a fake gun out of wood or someone slipped him a gun during a visit. Either way, he was on the loose. A few months later, he was shot and killed by FBI agents outside of the Biograph Theatre in Chicago.

The old jail and sheriff's house is now maintained by a non-profit organization that gives tours of the historic building on Saturday's during the summer months. You can learn more at their website:
www.oldsheriffshouse.org.

Octave Chanute

 6918 Oak Ave.
Gary, IN 46403
41.619844928820655, -87.25711452214307

The historic Gary Bathing Beach Aquatorium stands along the Lake Michigan shoreline in the Indiana Dunes. It was constructed in 1921 and saved from the wrecking ball by a local non-profit group that restored it. Atop a pole on the corner of the building is a curious-looking airplane with a manikin of a man hanging from it. It honors the memory of a man who influenced our modern world on the sand of the dunes.

Octave Chanute was a French-born civil engineer who emigrated to the United States in 1838 with his father when he was a young boy. Studying in New York, he became a prominent civil engineer and designed several significant bridges for the railroad. After witnessing a hot air balloon floating in the sky in 1856, he became interested in aviation.

Learning everything he could about airplanes, he began experimenting with designs of his own. In the 1890s, he was too old to pilot his aircraft himself; he partnered with younger experimenters, Augustus M. Herring and William Avery. They decided to test Chanute's designs in the winds off Lake

Michigan at the Indiana Dunes. They were strange-looking kite contraptions with a pilot hanging from the bottom. Many of the locals called Chanute "the crazy old man of the sand dunes".

Chanute willingly published his experiments in books and magazines of the day. He also corresponded with many aviation inventors in letters sharing his knowledge. He became friends with the Wright Brothers, and they wrote each other hundreds of letters.

Considered the godfather of aviation, Chanute not only pioneered early wing design, but he was also willing to propel the concept of flight forward by openly sharing his knowledge when most inventors work in secrecy. To honor his contribution to aviation and Indiana, a replica of one of his aircrafts sits atop the old bath house at the dunes. A portion of the bath house has been converted into a museum honoring his accomplishments.

On the other corner of the building is a World War II airplane painted to match the planes used by the Tuskegee Airmen. A section of the museum honors the achievement of the African American squadron.

Century of Progress Homes

The Florida Tropical Home

127 W Lake Front Dr.
Michigan City, IN 46360
41.68432988826889, -87.00175393556594

Along the Lake Michigan shoreline in the Indiana Dunes
National Park is a collection of five extraordinary houses. They
were built for the 1933 World's Fair in Chicago that was titled
The Century of Progress. Millions of people came to the fair
to marvel at the futuristic homes.

The houses were named the Florida Tropical, Rostone, Armco-Ferro, Cypress House and the House of Tomorrow, and showcased modern construction materials and techniques.

After the fair, Developer Robert Bartlett purchased the homes. He transported four of them by rolling them onto a barge using telephone poles. The Cypress house was dismantled and shipped by truck. He moved the houses to his Beverly Shores resort community. He hoped that the homes would garner attention to his development and boost sales. Unfortunately, the Great Depression hampered the sale of his homes.

The House of Tommorow in a state of repair.

In 1966, the National Park Service took over the area that included Beverly Shores, and it became part of the Indiana Dunes National Lakeshore. Homeowners became lessees; with little incentive to maintain the houses, they fell into a state of disrepair. The homes were eventually leased to Indiana Landmarks, which, in turn, did long term subleases to people willing to renovate them back to their former glory. Four of the houses have been restored with the House of Tomorrow being the final home to be completed. It is a unique octagon-shaped house with large windows. The first level was designed as an airplane hangar, thinking in the future everyone would have their own aircraft to fly for daily errands and commute to work.

Today the homes are used as private residences but can be viewed from the road. Once a year in the fall, the homes are opened to people to tour. Parking near the homes is limited, but there is a public parking lot for Dunbar Beach about one hundred yards west of the houses.

The Old Lighthouse

100 Heisman Harbor
Michigan City, IN 46360
41.722866277194846, -86.9060621509727

The second lighthouse in Michigan City was constructed in
1858. One of the most notable lighthouse keepers was Harriet
Colfax. She came to the Hoosier State in the 1850s with her
brother when they were both in their twenties. Her brother
was an editor of a newspaper, and she worked for him as a

typesetter. After his sudden death, she needed a job and she applied for a position as lightkeeper.

You know the old saying: "It's who you know and not what you know." That was the case with Harriet. Her cousin Schuyler Colfax was the Representative for Indiana in the United States House of Representatives. He was a successful and influential politician who eventually worked his way up to Speaker of the House and was vice president under Ulysses S. Grant. At the time, lighthouse keepers were appointed by the politicians in Washington D.C., and Schuyler arranged Harriet's appointment.

It is unclear if he ever mentioned that she was a woman, but Harriet became one of Michigan's most respected keepers. She tended the lights on the east and west piers for forty-three years. It was no easy task. Every night she had to row out to the light with kerosene fuel and light the lamp. She did this in all kinds of weather, from torrential thunderstorms in the spring to blinding snow storms and icy waves in the winter. She had help from her childhood friend Ann C. Hartwell, who lived with her in the Southern Lake Michigan Lighthouse. The two women retired in 1904 after decades of service and moved out of the government-owned lighthouse they had called home. About a year later, Ann died, and Harriet followed a few months later. The two women are buried next to each other in Michigan City's Greenwood Cemetery. The lighthouse was deactivated in 1904 and is now a museum.

The Train Wreck

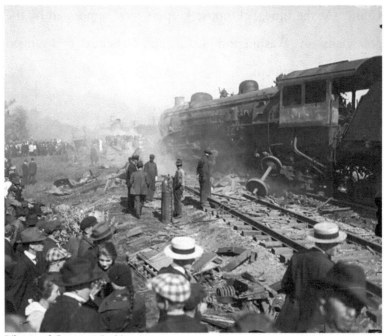

Library of Congress Archives.

The railroad tracks at the Indiana Illinois border near Hammond

The town of Hammond sits on the border between Indiana and Illinois a few miles south of Lake Michigan. Trains passed through the area on their way around the southern tip of Lake Michigan. It was near Hammond in the summer of 1918 that one of the worst train disasters took place.

At the turn of the century before movies and television, the circus was a major form of entertainment. They could be massive productions with hundreds of people from performers to laborers to put on a massive traveling show. The Hagenbeck–Wallace Circus was one of the largest in the nation and had an old train and railroad cars to transport its people and animals.

When passing through Hammond, the train stopped to check on some railroad cars for mechanical issues. Signals were set along the tracks to notify approaching locomotives of the stopped train up ahead. An empty transport train hauling passenger cars came into Hammond. The engineer had been operating the locomotive for nearly twenty-four hours and had fallen asleep and missed the signals. It slammed into the back of the circus train. Eighty-six people died, and another one hundred twenty-seven were injured. The wooden railroad cars were ignited by the lanterns and burned after the collision. Many of the bodies of the victims were unrecognizable.

A few months before the accident, a large lot of land was purchased in a cemetery in Forest Park, Illinois by the Showmen's League of America. Called the Showmen's Rest, it was surrounded by statues of elephants. The victims of the train wreck were laid to rest in the cemetery, and many of the unidentified graves were simply marked "Unknown Male" or "Unknown Female". As far as I know, there is no marker or memorial in Hammond recalling the tragic event. It remains as one of the worst railroad accidents in American history.

Orville Redenbacher

68 Lafayette St.
Valparaiso, IN 46383
41.46787647021945, -87.0619184067128

In Central Park Plaza in downtown Valparaiso is a bench with a bronze statue. It is of a man wearing a bow tie and glasses. If you have ever purchased popcorn at a grocery store you may recognize the statue as Orville Redenbacher. I think most people assume he was a made-up person by a clever marketing department and played by an actor. The truth is he was a remarkable man and was born in Indiana.

139

Born on a farm in Brazil, Indiana in 1907, It is believed his father named him after Orvill Wright of the Wright Brothers because he marveled at their accomplishments and he liked the name. Orville went on to Purdue University and studied agriculture. After graduating, he worked for a company selling fertilizer. He soon partnered with his friend Charlie Bowman and they purchased George F. Chester and Son seed corn plant in Boone Grove, Indiana.

During World War II, sugar was rationed and popcorn became a popular treat. At the time, corn kernels did not pop well or even at all. Charlie and Orville saw an opportunity and worked tirelessly at growing the best corn for popping. They crossed hybrid strains of corn, creating thousands of different varieties until they found the perfect kernel for popping. Originally, it was marketed as Redbow Popcorn, using a combination of both or their last names. A marketing agency suggested they use Orvill's name and likeness on their packaging.

Redenbacher had worn a large bow tie for years, and his dark rimmed glasses and wavy gray hair added to his unique look. The two men made a superior popcorn, and when the consumer market took off in the fifties with televisions, invading many American homes, they looked to homemade popcorn for an easy snack. It was Orville's image that stood out in the popcorn aisle, and he promised the best popping corn you could buy. Orville died in 1995. In 2012, Valparaiso unveiled a statue of Redenbacher at the city's annual popcorn festival.

Redenbacher claimed that people would send him letters with a kernel of popcorn in it. They wrote that the kernel did not pop. He said he graciously mailed them a new kernel back.

Roadside Memorial

N. 400 E. south of E.700 N.
Lake Village, IN 46349
41.09648429051021, -87.31423613523037

Next to a seldom used road in the farmland around Fair Oaks
is a brick and stone memorial. It is for American Eagle Flight
4184 that crashed in the field, killing all sixty-eight people on
board. The airplane left from Indianapolis on a cold and rainy

Halloween Day in 1994. It was headed for Chicago but placed in a holding pattern before it could land because of weather delays.

The wings began to ice over and the pilots lost control of the aircraft. They desperately tried to regain control, but it violently slammed into the Indiana soybean field at over four hundred miles per hour. It was difficult to recover and identify the victims because of the force of the impact. This memorial was erected to remember the people's lives that ended and stands as a reminder of that tragic day.

A few miles to the south of the memorial is the Fair Oaks Dairy farm, one of the largest dairy farms in the country.

Fort Wayne's Fort

1201 Spy Run Ave.
Fort Wayne, IN 46805
41.08535638681608, -85.13623190671444

I traveled through Fort Wayne, and near the river I saw a large historic fort. I was not surprised to see it since I figured the town got its start as a military fort. I was surprised to learn that it was one of several forts to occupy the land near the river. The location was of great importance because it is the junction of the St. Mary's, St. Joseph, and Maumee Rivers. Goods could travel by boat from Toledo along Lake Erie down to the Gulf Of Mexico with a short portage and the junction of the three rivers.

The French and British were the first to build forts at this location. The fifth and final military fort was built in 1815. It was one of the most well-designed wooden forts built in North America. It was built to defend and protect against attacks by Native Americans and named after General "Mad" Anthony Wayne. Shortly after it was constructed and after the end of the War of 1812, the fighting with the Native Americans subsided, and Fort Wayne was decommissioned in 1819.

The area was still important to commerce, and the city eventually grew around the old fort. The last remaining portion was razed in 1852. In the 1960s a non profit group raised funds to build a replica of the old fort. Construction was completed, and it officially opened on July 4, 1976 in honor of the nation's Bicentennial. Known as The Old Fort, it is maintained by a nonprofit organization and is a great place to step back in time to the early days of the United States. I have visited other replicas of forts in that era, but I will say the one at Fort Wayne is impressive at how large it is.

The Old Fort is located in a public park, and the grounds are open year round. The buildings are only open during events. You can find more info at www.oldfortwayne.org.

Philo's House

734 E. State Blvd.
Fort Wayne, IN 46805
41.0965103034756, -85.13028910879554

North of downtown Fort Wayne near Northside Park is a pale yellow house with white trim and a picket fence. A historical marker lets people know it was the home of Philo T. Farnsworth. Most people know the names of famous inventors like Thomas Edison, Alexander Graham Bell or the Wright Brothers, but few people know about Farnsworth, although they use his invention for hours every day.

He was born in 1906 in Utah. At a young age, his family moved to a farm in Idaho. The farm had a generator to provide electricity; as a young boy, Philo became fascinated with it. At the age of fourteen, he was plowing the field and thought about using electricity to transmit images in rows like the plowing of a field. He made a sketch of a vacuum tube for a television for his high school science teacher.

His family moved back to Utah, and Phio attended Brigham Young University but dropped out after his father died of pneumonia. With funding from a friend, he moved to San Francisco and set up a lab and introduced the first all-electronic television in 1927 while he was in his early twenties. He was given an offer from RCA but turned it down. They remained in litigation over the patent rights to television for over a decade. He finally won his case with the drawing that he created for his high school teacher. Thankfully, his teacher had held onto it.

With the money he got from RCA for licensing rights in 1938, Farnsworth established the Farnsworth Television and Radio Corporation in Fort Wayne, Indiana. In 1951, it was purchased by International Telephone and Telegraph; most people just know it as ITT. During his time at ITT, Farnsworth worked in the basement of a building on Pontiac Street. His laboratory was known as "the cave", and there he worked on several more inventions, including radar innovations used in air traffic control.

Farnsworth died in Utah fighting a bout of pneumonia in 1971 at the age of 64, never gaining fame or fortune from his invention. He was frustrated with his battles with RCA and never watched his invention much. As he watched the moon landing in 1969 on TV, he turned to his wife, who had helped him with his research over the years, and said, "This has made it all worthwhile." In 2010, the former Farnsworth factory in Fort Wayne, Indiana, was razed, but his home still stands; it is privately owned.

The *Futurama* character Professor Farnsworth, is named after and was partially inspired by Philo Farnsworth. In the episode "All the Presidents' Heads" it was revealed the Professor Farnsworth descended from Philo.

Studebaker Mansion

620 W. Washington St.
South Bend, IN 46601
41.6757979309914, -86.25796206644249

The largest and most opulent house in South Bend stands a
few blocks west of downtown. It was built in 1889 by Clement
Studebaker. If you are a Baby Boomer, you will probably
recognize the name Studebaker. If you are considerably
younger, you might not know that it was the name of an

automobile company. Most people probably don't know that the company started long before the invention of the automobile.

In 1852, Clement Studebaker and his older brother Henry opened the H. & C. Studebaker blacksmith shop. It stood at the corner of Michigan and Jefferson Streets in what is now the heart of downtown South Bend. They began making wagons and during the Civil War supplied wagons to the Union Army. With the help of Clements three other brothers, the Studebaker Brothers Manufacturing Company went on to become the largest manufacturer of wagons in the United States. In the early 1900s, the company transitioned to manufacturing automobiles. After World War II, the company struggled and produced its last automobile in 1963. Not much of the company remains in South Bend other than the home of Clement Studebaker.

It is a massive four-story stone house. It has forty rooms and twenty fireplaces. It took almost four years to construct at a cost of a quarter million dollars. Eight months after the home was completed, the upper floors were destroyed by a fire. Another hundred thousand dollars were spent to repair the damages. Clement lived in the home until he died in 1901. His son lived in the home until 1933, when he lost it due to bankruptcy. The home sat empty for almost a decade until it was used by the Red Cross during World War II. After the war, it was used as a school for disabled children. In the 1970s, the home was restored to its former glory by a historic preservation group, and it currently operates as a restaurant and brewery.

> The Studebaker Museum is located a few blocks to the west at 201 Chapin St. It is home to the world's largest collection of U.S. Presidential Carriages. The collection features the Barouche that President Abraham Lincoln used the night of his assassination, President Grant's Brewster Landau, President McKinley's Studebaker Phaeton, and President Benjamin Harrison's Studebaker Brougham.The museum also has more than thirty Studebaker automobiles on display.

Meshingomesia School

2820 W. 600 N.
Marion, IN 46952
40.640851799267665, -85.73046759127811

The Mississinewa River flows through the farmland between Kokomo and Fort Wayne. In the 1840s, Chief Meshingomesia of the Miami of Indiana negotiated a reservation with the United States. In 1860, a school was built along the river to educate the Miami children and assimilate them into American culture. By 1898, the school was no longer used and some of the reservation had been sold by the Chiefs ancestors. By the 1930s, the old school was being used as a corn crib.

After Chief Meshingomesia died in 1879, he was buried in a plot of land along with thirty other people who had died from a tuberculosis outbreak. In the 1990s, the owner of the farm where the old school now stood donated it to the leaders of the Miami of Indiana. It was dismantled and moved to the cemetery where it was restored and now stands. Today it is used to educate Americans about the Miami of Indiana's culture.

The schoolhouse is open one weekend a year in late October to the public during the annual commemoration of the War of 1812 battle on the Mississinewa River. You can learn more at their website www.miamiindians.org.

Oliver Mansion

808 W. Washington St.
South Bend, IN 46601
41.67599619514981, -86.26207091959172

Next to the Studebaker Museum in South Bend is an enormous stone mansion. Known as the Oliver Mansion, it was home to a family that has historic roots in Indiana. James Oliver was born in Scotland in 1823. At a young age, he emigrated with his family to the United States and ended up on a farm in Indiana. He worked the fields and in local foundries, gaining knowledge of casting metal.

In the 1850s, he partnered with a couple other men to purchase a foundry in South Bend. He patented a plow that was stronger than others because he came up with a technique of chilling the edge of the plow when it was cast that made for a better plow. Oliver manufactured a plow he called the "Indiana Plow". With its strong sales, he used the money to buy out his partners, making him the sole owner of the company. He continued making plows and agricultural equipment, and the company became one of the largest suppliers of farm implements in the country. His son Joseph D. Oliver took over the company after his death and went on to build tractors. The company built Oliver tractors until the 1960s when it merged with White Motor Company.

In 1895, With the success of the Oliver Farm Equipment Company, J.D. Oliver built his mansion in South Bend. Calling it Copshaholm in honor of his father's birthplace in Scotland, the home had thirty eight rooms and was one of the first homes in Indiana to be wired for electricity. After J.D. died in 1933, his four children lived in the home. The Oliver family decided that it should be used as a museum, and in the late 1960s it was turned over to the Northern Indiana Historical Society. The home still has all its original woodwork, decor and furnishings.

Lincoln Highway

Original Marker
545 N. Lake St.
Warsaw, IN 46580
41.24305708553187, -85.86027030777153

Ideal Section
1250 Joliet St.
Dyer, IN 46311
41.49155479330161, -87.49751342215417

North Lake Street in Warsaw, Indiana passes by Funk Park. There you will notice a stone marker surrounded by a wrought iron fence. It has a faded red, white, and blue mark along with an arrow and a round medallion of Abraham Lincoln's face. It is one of the original markers for the Lincoln Highway. It was the first transcontinental road that linked New York and San Francisco. The road may start in those cities, but the concept of the cross-country road began in Indiana.

The road was proposed by Indiana native and co-founder of the Indianapolis Motor Speedway Carl G. Fisher. It was challenging traveling on dirt wagon roads between towns and cities in the early days of the automobile and nearly impossible when it rained. As the automobile gained in popularity, the need for better roads became evident.

On July 1, 1913, the Lincoln Highway Association was established and led by Carl Fisher. After a route was established, the association raised funds to build the road. It did not have enough money to build the entire road, so it built "seedling miles" which were short segments to show travelers a well paved road can be a joy to drive on. The association needed to determine the best type of road to build that would last for more than twenty years. After contacting several engineers, specifications were set. The first seedling mile with the new requirements was laid down in the Indian town of Dyer near the Illinois border. It became known as the "ideal section" and set the standard for the rest of the Lincoln Highway which was completed in 1928. In the 1950s, the U.S. adopted a numbering system for interstate roads and most of the Lincoln Highway that passes through Indiana became US-30.

In the town of Dyer, a stone monument stands next to the Ideal Section. It is also a memorial to Henry C. Ostermann, vice-president of the Lincoln Highway Association, who was killed on the Lincoln Highway in Iowa in 1920.

Conclusion

I enjoyed my time traveling through Indiana. I was surprised by the early American history that I learned. It was also interesting to see the change in scenery from the farmland in the north to the hills and forests along the Ohio River Valley in the south. One thing I noticed on my trip is the American flag waving over many cemeteries, parks and buildings. It reminds me of how lucky I am to live in a country where I am free to roam and explore.

I hope you enjoyed reading this book and are inspired to get lost in Indiana.

I hope you will continue
to follow my journey at

www.lostinthestates.com

Other Books by Mike Sonnenberg

Lost In Michigan Volumes 1-6

Lost In Ohio

Light From The Birdcage

Made in United States
Troutdale, OR
10/28/2023

14084890R10096